Digital Real Estate & Virtual Assets

How to Buy, Flip, or Rent Property in the Metaverse and Build Long-Term Wealth

By Joe Correa

Published by Live Stronger Faster

This book is for educational and informational purposes only. The author and publisher are not engaged in rendering legal, financial, or other professional advice. Readers should consult a qualified professional before making any financial decisions.

First Edition

Table of Contents

Introduction

The idea of owning land in a world that doesn't physically exist may sound futuristic, strange, or even unnecessary at first glance. Yet if we look at history, this phenomenon is neither new nor surprising. Every major technological shift has created new forms of property, wealth, and ownership that once seemed ridiculous—until people realized they were life-changing opportunities. When radio first emerged, companies spent fortunes buying invisible frequencies in the air. When the internet became mainstream, domain names—simple strings of characters—sold for millions. Social media usernames became valuable digital real estate for brands and celebrities. And today, as millions of people migrate into virtual spaces where they socialize, work, attend events, learn, shop, and play, a new form of prime location has emerged: **digital land and virtual assets.**

What makes this moment different from past shifts is the scale and speed at which the digital economy is evolving. The metaverse is no longer a hypothetical vision or a gaming world for teenagers. It is becoming a fully-fledged digital ecosystem where businesses launch storefronts, creators build communities, brands host global events, artists exhibit work, influencers monetize experiences, and everyday investors acquire high-value property that appreciates over time. Digital real estate has rapidly become one of the most lucrative – and misunderstood – opportunities in the Web3 revolution. Just like physical real estate, virtual land is limited, location-dependent, utility-driven, community-powered, and influenced by trends, infrastructure, and long-term adoption. But unlike physical real estate, it is borderless, infinitely customizable, instantly transferable, and capable of producing income streams that have no traditional-world equivalent. This book exists to guide you through this new territory and show you how you can safely, intelligently, and profitably participate in the digital property boom.

Digital real estate in the metaverse includes far more than parcels of virtual land. It encompasses storefronts, rental units, event spaces, training grounds, advertising billboards, gaming arenas, social hubs, VIP clubs, branded districts, experience centers, learning environments, and anything else that can be constructed in a 3D digital world. It also includes virtual assets such as wearables, tools, digital furniture, vehicles, collectible items, in-game resources, and even AI-powered characters who can generate income. In a decentralized environment powered by blockchain, these assets are not merely files—they are verifiable, ownable, tradeable, rent-able, and programmed to produce cash flow.

They are investments, and some of them have already made early adopters millions.

But how do you evaluate something that cannot be touched? What truly gives digital land value? Why do some parcels sell for tens of thousands while others sit empty for years? The answers lie in a blend of economics, community psychology, user experience design, game theory, branding, and blockchain technology. Digital real estate becomes valuable for the same core reasons that physical property becomes valuable: location, demand, scarcity, infrastructure, planned development, and the commercial opportunity it enables. Yet unlike physical real estate, a piece of digital land can become valuable simply because a popular creator builds next door, a major brand announces a partnership, or a cultural moment drives millions of people into a particular world. Digital real estate reacts quickly, grows quickly, and can be monetized in dozens of ways that traditional property cannot.

The purpose of this book is to break down this ecosystem in a practical, beginner-friendly, and financially strategic way. You will learn how digital land is created, how it is divided, how ownership works, and how decentralization ensures that what you purchase is genuinely yours. We will explore the most important metaverse platforms—Decentraland, The Sandbox, Otherside, Voxels, Spatial, Meta Horizon, Roblox, and emerging worlds—and compare their economies, builder tools, rental markets, land mechanics, and long-term growth potential. This book will walk you through how to analyze neighborhoods, evaluate demand, assess risk, identify undervalued parcels, and spot upcoming districts that could become valuable hubs in the future. You will learn exactly how to buy digital land, how to flip it, how to rent it, how to develop it into a business, and how to diversify into other virtual assets that complement your portfolio.

Perhaps the most exciting aspect of digital real estate is that it democratizes opportunity. In the physical world, buying property often requires a large down payment, financing, inspections, and recurring expenses. In the metaverse, you can start with low-cost assets, fractional ownership, micro-rentals, or virtual developments that cost a fraction of traditional construction. You can test ideas instantly, modify them freely, and scale them without limits. You can build an art gallery, a virtual school, a coaching center, a gaming experience, a branded event venue, an online store, or a community hub—without hiring contractors, buying furniture, or waiting for permits. The metaverse gives you tools that allow creativity to become commerce.

This book will also show you the biggest risks, mistakes, and myths surrounding digital real estate. Yes, there is hype in this space—but behind the hype is a genuine shift in how humans interact with digital environments. The winners in Web3 will be those who understand value, strategy, timing, and utility—not those chasing trends. You will learn how to protect your assets, avoid inflated markets, identify sustainable long-term investments, and create digital properties that generate recurring income. Whether you are a complete beginner with no metaverse experience or an entrepreneur looking to diversify into new income streams, this book will give you the blueprint you need.

By the time you finish this introduction and move into the core chapters, you will understand why digital real estate is not a passing fad but a transformative new category of wealth creation. You will learn how people are already making six and seven figures through flipping parcels, building virtual businesses, hosting immersive events, renting commercial space to brands, selling digital assets, and creating Web3 experiences that attract global audiences. You will see how the next decade will reshape online identity, work, commerce, education, entertainment, and investment—and why early participants will have enormous advantages.

This is your guide to stepping into the next frontier of digital opportunity. You are about to learn how digital property works, how to profit from it, how to build a long-term virtual portfolio, and how to position yourself early in a market that will define Web 3.0. As you turn the page, remember this: all wealth begins with understanding the landscape before the rest of the world recognizes it. You are not just reading about digital real estate—you are preparing to own a piece of the future.

Chapter 1

The Foundations of Digital Real Estate

Digital real estate may be virtual, but the principles behind it are surprisingly grounded in traditional economics, psychology, and community-driven value creation. Before you can buy, flip, rent, or develop digital property, you must understand how and why digital land exists, what gives it value, and how metaverse platforms design their economies. At its core, digital real estate is a fusion of blockchain ownership, gaming mechanics, virtual world infrastructure, and decentralized property rights. Unlike intangible digital items from past internet generations, Web3 assets are verifiable, traceable, scarce, and transferable. That single shift—provable digital ownership—turns virtual spaces into investable assets. Chapter 1 lays the foundation: how digital land is created, why platforms limit supply, what drives value, and why digital property is quickly becoming one of the most forward-looking wealth opportunities in Web 3.0.

The first key concept is **digital scarcity**, which is entirely intentional. In the physical world, land is scarce because Earth is finite. In the digital world, scarcity is programmed by platform creators. They could technically mint unlimited land parcels, but they don't, because scarcity is what creates economic value, community identity, and investment potential. For example, Decentraland has exactly 90,601 parcels, permanently capped by the blockchain. The Sandbox has 166,464 parcels. Otherside, the Yuga Labs metaverse, has a limited supply of "Otherdeeds." Each number is fixed, and each parcel has coordinates, size, and metadata that define its uniqueness. Scarcity prevents the digital economy from collapsing into oversupply and gives early buyers the same advantage early landowners have always had: limited competition and predictable future appreciation.

The second pillar is **location**, which matters in the metaverse just as much as in the physical world—sometimes even more. Popular districts, high-traffic hubs, celebrity-owned parcels, branded experiences, gaming arenas, and commercial centers drive value. In Decentraland, land near Genesis Plaza or celebrity districts often sells for more. In The Sandbox, parcels next to brands like Snoop Dogg, Adidas, Atari, and The Walking Dead command premium prices. The metaverse still has neighborhoods, districts, pathways, and central plazas—only theirs are digital. Location determines visibility, rental demand, traffic flow, and long-term relevance. Understanding location strategy is one of the most important skills in digital real estate investing.

A third key principle is **utility**, which drives sustainable value far more than aesthetics. Utility refers to how the land can be used: building a business, creating a game, hosting events, renting space, constructing a gallery, launching a training center, or running interactive experiences. Land without utility rarely grows in value long-term. A digital parcel with strong utility can become an income-producing asset worth multiples of its original price. In the metaverse, utility is often tied to platform-specific tools such as builder kits, game creation engines, event systems, avatar interactions, NFT integration, and monetization options. When evaluating land, always ask: How can this land produce value? What can happen here that people will visit, join, pay for, or share?

Then comes **community**, which is arguably the strongest long-term value driver in Web3. A metaverse world with millions of active users, strong creators, profitable businesses, and major brand partnerships will always offer better investment conditions than a world with small or stagnant user growth. Digital real estate value is community-powered. If the community grows, the economy grows. If builders, creators, and investors collaborate to produce immersive experiences, the land appreciates. In this way, buying digital real estate is similar to buying stock in the platform's cultural and economic future. You are not only buying a parcel—you are buying into a world. The fifth principle is **ownership**

verification, enabled by blockchain technology. Every parcel is a token—usually an NFT—on a specific blockchain (Ethereum, Polygon, Solana, etc.). Ownership cannot be altered, deleted, or counterfeited. When you buy land, you control the asset through your wallet. The platform does not own your land; you do. This also allows you to sell your parcel on open marketplaces, rent it out through smart contracts, or transfer it to another wallet instantly. The blockchain replaces the need for middlemen, escrow companies, title agents, or banks. Digital property is frictionless, transparent, and globally transferable.

To fully understand digital real estate, you must also understand **platform economies**. Each metaverse world has its own currency, marketplace, builder tools, zoning system, rental mechanics, and economic incentives. Decentraland uses MANA. The Sandbox uses SAND. Otherside uses APE. These tokens often govern land purchases, staking rewards, governance voting, creator payments, and platform transactions. In this chapter, you'll learn how to evaluate the financial health of a platform by analyzing user activity, developer tools, transaction volume, roadmap credibility, brand partnerships, and token utility. Economic strength determines whether your investment appreciates or stagnates.

A seventh foundational concept is **development potential**. Some parcels appreciate simply because they are near valuable districts, but the highest ROI often comes from what you *build* on your land. A gamer who builds a play-to-earn experience may earn more than a landlord who simply holds undeveloped land. A creator who builds an art gallery or training center can generate recurring rental income. A brand that builds an events venue may use it to host thousands of visitors monthly. Digital land becomes a canvas for business creation—many investors underestimate this and miss massive opportunities.

Next, you must grasp **interoperability**, the ability for assets, avatars, or experiences to move or connect between worlds. While not all metaverse platforms are interoperable yet, the long-term trend is clear: users want unified digital identities, transferable assets, and cross-world experiences. When evaluating land, consider platforms that invest in open standards, partnerships, and NFT ecosystems that support cross-platform functionality.

Finally, the foundation of digital real estate requires understanding **long-term adoption cycles**. Just like early internet real estate (domains, early websites, keyword-based properties), the metaverse will experience waves of volatility. Early markets rise fast, dip hard, consolidate, and expand again as adoption grows. The goal is not to time the hype; it is to position yourself for the long-term trend. Digital real estate is a generational opportunity aligned with how people increasingly live, work, and socialize online. The more the metaverse becomes a place where people gather, learn, earn, and create, the more valuable digital property becomes. Chapter 1 is your introduction to these foundational principles so that every strategy in the rest of the book is built upon a strong understanding of value mechanics, economic structure, and long-term opportunity.

"The Plot Next to Genesis Plaza"

Elias never imagined he would become a landowner in a world made of pixels. At 42, he was a careful investor—conservative, analytical, more comfortable with spreadsheets than with video game avatars. But on a quiet evening in 2029, he logged into Decentraland for the first time after hearing a friend mention that a virtual plot near Genesis Plaza had sold for more than a small condo in Florida. At first, he laughed. Then he walked his avatar forward. And everything changed.

Genesis Plaza stretched out like a glowing metropolis floating beneath a digital sky. Billboards flickered. Avatars teleported in flashes of blue. Music pulsed from a virtual club in the distance. Elias watched a group of friends take selfies beside a waterfall that didn't exist in the real world. A creator ran past him wearing floating neon wings. A DJ streamed live music from his bedroom in New York while hundreds danced in sync. Suddenly, this world didn't feel like a game. It felt like a city—a real, living city with neighborhoods, energy, commerce, and opportunity.

Elias walked to the edge of the plaza, noticing parcels lined in perfect grid patterns, each one bordered by glowing outlines. Some were empty fields waiting to be developed. Others had towering structures: galleries, storefronts, offices, lounges, studios. A small popup window told him the coordinates, parcel ID, owner wallet, and purchase history. Digital land wasn't just property—it was data, transparent and open to everyone. He clicked another parcel and saw its last sale price. His eyebrows rose. People were buying and selling these spaces every day.

He spent hours walking the world. Every district had a mood: Fashion Street with its runways and holograms, Vegas City with neon casinos, the Museum Quarter with art that could never exist physically. He began noticing something important: the busiest areas weren't random. They were close to portals, plazas, and major attractions. The same logic he used for physical real estate—foot traffic, proximity, demand—applied here too. This was a city governed by digital rules but grounded in familiar economics.

The next day, he returned to the coordinates he had bookmarked: a small but promising parcel just two units from the Genesis Plaza border. It wasn't extravagant, but it had location—and in real estate, digital or not, location always wins. The listing price was higher than he expected. His logical mind resisted. But he remembered the traffic he saw, the energy in the plaza, the brands building here. He imagined creating a small learning center where newcomers could understand blockchain basics, join events, or take onboarding tours. He didn't need construction crews or permits—just creativity and builder tools. The idea began to feel real.

He clicked "Buy." His heart pounded as the blockchain transaction processed. In seconds, the plot belonged to him—verifiable, recorded, undeniable. He stared at the empty parcel, imagining what it could become. For the first time in years, he felt the thrill of being early to something big.

Weeks passed. Elias experimented with different builds: a small info booth, a hologram display, a lounge. He eventually created a sleek glass-walled learning center with floating screens, interactive tutorials, and an AI-powered guide. At first, only a handful of people visited each day. But traffic from Genesis Plaza spilled over. Then creators began referencing his center in community chat. Then influencers brought their followers for tours. And then a brand approached him about renting the space for a week-long onboarding event.

One evening, Elias stood in his digital center watching dozens of avatars explore the exhibits he had built. A sense of pride washed over him—not because he owned virtual land, but because he had created value in a world where anyone could build anything. He had taken a risk, believed in a frontier no one fully understood yet, and turned a simple digital parcel into something meaningful.

As he walked outside, the neon skyline shimmered. The plaza buzzed with activity. And Elias realized something profound: the metaverse wasn't the future—it was the present. Digital real estate wasn't imaginary. It was a new form of ownership, a new kind of business, and a new path to wealth. And he was standing on plot #42-19, the small piece of digital soil that started it all.

Chapter 2

Understanding Metaverse Platforms & Land Systems

Before you invest a single dollar into digital real estate, you must understand the platforms that define the metaverse landscape. Each world has its own rules, economy, tools, culture, user base, and growth trajectory. Just like physical real estate markets—Miami, New York, Austin, Dubai—each metaverse platform has different levels of demand, different risk profiles, and different profit opportunities. The key to profitable investing is understanding not only *what* to buy but *where* to buy it. Chapter 2 is your guide to the four major categories of metaverse platforms, how land systems work within each one, and how to analyze the underlying mechanics that determine long-term value.

The first category is **decentralized blockchain metaverses**, the most investment-focused environments in Web3. Examples include Decentraland, The Sandbox, Otherside, Voxels, Somnium Space, and NFT Worlds (now reemerging with a builder ecosystem). These worlds are built on blockchain, meaning land parcels are NFTs, ownership is permanent and verifiable, and marketplaces are open. Decentralized metaverses typically have fixed land supplies, established district maps, community-governed economies, and token-based financial systems. Here, real digital real estate strategies—flipping, renting, developing, and long-term holding—are most effective. Investors are drawn to these worlds because they combine scarcity with creator tools and long-term community value.

The second category is **corporate or centralized metaverses**, such as Meta Horizon Worlds, Fortnite Creative, Roblox, and Rec Room. These platforms usually have larger user bases but do not always offer land ownership. Instead, they provide creative spaces where builders can create games, experiences, and environments without purchasing parcels. While they lack the NFT-based ownership of decentralized platforms, they offer massive attention, strong monetization systems, and a proven track record of high engagement. Fortnite Creative maps regularly bring in millions of players; Roblox games earn creators millions in payments; Meta Horizon Worlds hosts official brand events. Even without land ownership mechanics, these platforms are important because they influence mainstream adoption and future Web3 migration.

The third category is **hybrid metaverses**, which combine digital ownership with centralized infrastructure. Platforms like Spatial, Mona, Nifty Island, and OnCyber fall into this group. They allow creators to own NFTs representing worlds or environments but host them in centralized servers with enhanced visual quality and frictionless onboarding. Hybrid worlds often grow quickly because they offer a smoother user experience while still supporting ownership. These platforms are ideal for creators who want to build galleries, shops, events, or immersive spaces without navigating the complexities of large land maps or high land prices. While their economies are newer, their potential is significant.

The fourth category is **emerging AI-driven metaverses**, which use artificial intelligence to generate worlds, NPCs, content, and experiences. Early examples include Inworld AI, AI World Labs, and experimental builder platforms that let users create environments in seconds through natural language prompts. AI-driven metaverses will dramatically expand the creation and customization possibilities, reducing development costs and enabling users to build large-scale environments without coding or design knowledge. As these platforms mature, digital land demand may shift toward worlds that blend AI assets, metaverse interoperability, and creator monetization.

Understanding land systems is equally essential. Digital land typically falls into several key formats. The most common is the **grid-based system**, used by Decentraland and The

Sandbox. Land exists in fixed coordinates, similar to a city map. Parcel adjacency matters, road proximity matters, and district clustering shapes value. Another system is **open world parcels**, where land is not locked to a strict grid but placed in a dynamic map, such as Somnium Space's terrain-based plots. Some platforms use **world NFTs**, where users own entire 3D environments rather than individual land parcels, common in Spatial or Mona. This offers more freedom but less traditional "neighborhood value." Others use **islands, zones, or plots** with thematic layouts, particularly in gaming-focused environments.

When evaluating a platform, analyze **supply mechanics**. How many parcels exist? Is the supply fixed forever? Does governance control future expansion? Worlds with unlimited or unregulated land supply risk dilution—making early parcels worth less over time. On the other hand, worlds with fixed scarcity tend to reward long-term holders. Always check: "Is the platform committed to keeping land scarce, or is expansion a part of its roadmap?"

Next, evaluate **utility infrastructure**. What can you build? Are there no-code tools? Can you host events? Can you design buildings? Is there scripting support? Are experiences interactive or purely visual? The Sandbox offers VoxEdit and Game Maker for interactive game design. Decentraland has builder kits, SDKs, and event frameworks. Spatial allows world creation with stunning visuals and drag-and-drop functionality. Utility drives demand; if creators cannot build compelling experiences, land value stagnates.

A third essential framework is **user base analysis**. Even a great platform with strong tools requires active users. Look at monthly active users (MAU), community engagement, brand partnerships, event frequency, creator adoption, and interoperability initiatives. Do brands build here? Do creators earn money here? Are users returning regularly or just experimenting? A platform with strong culture and sticky experiences will always outperform a visually impressive world with minimal activity.

Fourth is **economic stability**. What is the platform's token? How is it used? Is it inflationary or deflationary? Are there staking incentives? Does land pricing correlate with token value? Has the platform raised funding or signed major partnerships? In decentralized worlds, token stability affects land affordability, development budgets, and long-term investor confidence.

Finally, consider **roadmap credibility**. Many metaverse platforms promote grand visions, but only a handful consistently deliver updates. Evaluate the leadership, team transparency, development pace, governance structure, and history of executing promised features. Worlds that evolve consistently tend to appreciate consistently.

Understanding platforms and land systems is the foundation of smart digital real estate investing. By mastering how worlds differ, how land is structured, and how economies function, you gain the ability to identify opportunities before the masses. In the metaverse, timing and understanding are everything. Chapter 2 gives you the knowledge to choose the right worlds, analyze their stability, and position yourself where growth is inevitable.

"The Tour Through Worlds"

When Sofia first heard people talk about "buying land in the metaverse," she imagined a single massive world—one giant digital city where everyone gathered. But as she soon discovered, the metaverse wasn't one world. It was countless worlds, each with its own culture, economy, and rhythm. Her journey began the day she joined the "World Explorer Tour," a live guided event hosted by a popular creator named Zephyr.

The moment she logged in, a vibrant portal room appeared around her—dozens of glowing gates floating in the air, each representing a different metaverse. "Welcome, travelers," Zephyr's voice echoed. "Today, we visit the worlds where the future is being built." A dozen avatars stood beside Sofia, their names hovering above their heads. Some wore designer skins; others were simple default characters. But they all shared the same curiosity.

The first portal opened with a soft hum: **Decentraland**. The group stepped through. Suddenly they stood in a vast cityscape where every corner hummed with activity. Music spilled from clubs, digital art filled the streets, and screens displayed upcoming events. "This," Zephyr explained, "is one of the first decentralized worlds. Land is permanently scarce. Ownership is real. Everything here is powered by community." Sofia watched as a creator placed pixel blocks in mid-air, building a new shop in real time. The sight was mesmerizing. It wasn't just digital art—it was construction with no limits.

The next portal took them to **The Sandbox**, where the world looked more stylized—blocky, vibrant, full of energy. A massive Snoop Dogg statue towered over a district filled with branded venues. "This world," Zephyr said, "is built for creators. Tools for games, events, and interactive experiences are everywhere." She watched a group test a new platformer game on a floating island. A digital dog chased them playfully. It felt like Disneyland built by gamers.

Their next stop was **Otherside**, the sprawling world built by

Yuga Labs. The sky here glowed with shifting auroras, and floating islands drifted in the distance. Sofia felt a sense of awe—this world was alive in a way she had never seen. "Otherside is ambitious," Zephyr said quietly. "It's meant to be a universe, not just a world." A massive creature roared in the distance while adventurers rode flying creatures across bioluminescent forests. This world felt like magic mixed with technology.

From there, they entered **Spatial**, a hybrid platform known for its breathtaking visuals. The environment resembled a luxury art gallery floating above the ocean. Waves shimmered below as creators displayed digital sculptures. "Here," Zephyr said, "people own rooms and worlds, but not through land parcels. It's more fluid—perfect for creators, educators, and designers." Sofia walked through a gallery displaying NFT art from global creators. The artwork seemed alive, shifting and evolving as she approached.

The tour continued through Roblox, Horizon Worlds, Voxels, and a handful of emerging, AI-generated landscapes. Each world had its identity. Some felt playful. Some felt corporate. Some felt like thriving cities. Others felt like quiet towns waiting for pioneers. Sofia realized something important: digital real estate wasn't about buying land—it was about choosing a *world*. A culture. A community. A future. Near the end of the tour, Zephyr guided them to a viewing platform floating between portals. “Now that you’ve seen the worlds,” he said, “you must choose based on your goals. Are you here to build? To invest? To socialize? To create? Each world rewards different mindsets.”

Sofia stood silently, processing everything she had seen. She thought of Decentraland’s bustling streets, The Sandbox’s creative playground, Otherside’s breathtaking landscapes, Spatial’s elegance. She imagined building a retreat center in Spatial or a mini-game in The Sandbox. She imagined buying a parcel near a popular district in Decentraland and renting it out during the next global event.

“This,” Zephyr said softly, “is the real beginning. The metaverse is not one place. It is many places. And each one is writing a different part of the future.”

As the portals dimmed and the group prepared to leave, Sofia felt something she hadn’t felt in years—possibility. Boundless possibility. She realized that choosing the right world wasn’t just an investment decision; it was the first step in building her own digital legacy. And she knew, without question, that she would be back tomorrow to choose where her future would begin.

Chapter 3

How Digital Land Gets Its Value

Digital real estate may exist inside virtual worlds, but its value follows predictable and measurable economic patterns. Unlike random digital assets from past internet eras, Web3 property operates under structured market mechanics: scarcity, utility, community demand, token economics, cultural relevancy, and developer activity. Understanding how digital land gets its value is the difference between buying a high-potential asset and buying an overpriced parcel that never appreciates. In this chapter, you will learn the core valuation pillars, how to analyze price behavior, how to evaluate future potential, and how to identify undervalued land in growing worlds.

The first and most obvious value driver is **scarcity**, but scarcity alone does not guarantee growth. A platform may have a small number of parcels, but if the world is inactive or poorly maintained, scarcity becomes irrelevant. Effective scarcity is only meaningful when paired with active demand, strong development, and user interest. In top metaverse worlds, scarcity plays a powerful role. Decentraland and The Sandbox both have fixed land supplies, ensuring that early owners maintain long-term leverage. Otherside uses controlled land expansion tied to questing and gameplay mechanics. Scarcity determines potential appreciation, but only if the world has momentum.

The second—and often more important—value driver is **utility**, the ability to build, host, monetize, or develop something on the land. Utility turns digital real estate into a revenue-generating asset rather than a speculative collectible. A plot that can host events, run a game, showcase art, rent to a brand, or serve as a social hub naturally commands higher prices. Utility comes from two sources: platform tools (builder kits, SDKs, scripting tools, event systems) and community adoption (creators, businesses, brands). A world with strong tools but no community has limited utility; a world with a strong community but weak tools limits long-term creativity. You must evaluate both.

The third core valuation factor is **location**, which mirrors traditional real estate logic. High-traffic zones, plazas, portals, roadways, brand districts, gaming hubs, and cultural centers drive foot traffic. Even in digital spaces, humans gravitate toward central areas that feel populated, energetic, and relevant. Parcels near teleportation hubs, popular venues, celebrity estates, or branded districts almost always appreciate faster. Understanding a platform's map layout, planned expansions, neighborhood clusters, and event districts allows you to predict where value will concentrate.

A fourth major value driver is **community behavior**, which includes user activity, culture, social patterns, and engagement trends. A large user base doesn't always mean high land demand; what matters is how users interact with the world. Do they explore? Do they attend events? Do they visit businesses? Do creators build regularly? Do influencers promote experiences? Communities shape value by creating ongoing activity, attracting builders, and fostering world recognition. A passive community produces stagnant land markets; an active community produces compounding value.

Next is **economic ecosystem**, meaning how the platform's native token, marketplace, staking mechanisms, and revenue systems work. Land pricing often correlates with token value—if SAND rises, The Sandbox land prices typically rise; if MANA drops, Decentraland land becomes temporarily cheaper. Tokenomics also impact development: staking rewards may help creators fund their projects, and token utility encourages deeper world participation. An economy with clear purpose, strong liquidity, stable governance, and predictable inflation/deflation behaviors tends to support long-term land growth.

Another essential factor is **brand presence and partnerships**. When major companies, celebrities, or entertainment brands build inside a metaverse, surrounding land tends to appreciate. Adidas, Atari, Snoop Dogg, and The Walking Dead dramatically influenced The Sandbox pricing. JPMorgan, Samsung, and Sotheby's influenced Decentraland districts. In Otherside, the involvement of Yuga Labs alone creates cultural value. Brands bring attention, traffic, investors, creators, and legitimacy. Analyzing partnership announcements is a direct way to predict potential land appreciation.

The sixth value driver is **development momentum**, meaning how quickly creators, businesses, and neighborhoods evolve. In thriving areas, builders continuously add new structures, experiences, and attractions. These developments increase surrounding land value just as restaurants, parks, malls, or entertainment districts increase physical-world real estate. A stagnant region with undeveloped parcels or abandoned builds rarely appreciates. A lively district with constant updates becomes a long-term value engine.

A seventh factor is **experience quality**, which includes graphics, interactivity, immersion, sound design, and performance. While graphics alone do not create economic value, they determine user retention. The more immersive a world, the more time people spend there. The more time users spend, the more businesses, creators, and investors participate. And the more participation increases, the more valuable land becomes. Evaluating the long-term technical roadmap of a world is critical—platforms investing in optimization, VR integration, AI NPCs, and mobile accessibility tend to outperform those that do not.

One of the most overlooked value drivers is **cultural resonance**. Worlds become valuable when they represent a cultural movement, artistic community, gaming tribe, or generational identity. Voxels became a creative hub for artists. Roblox became a cultural hub for developers and youth. Otherside became the cultural home of the Bored Ape Yacht Club ecosystem. Cultural value is intangible but immensely powerful because it creates emotional attachment and long-term loyalty.

The final—and perhaps most predictive—value driver is **future vision**: the platform's roadmap, leadership, funding, strategic direction, and long-term goals. Not all worlds survive. Those with clear, consistent development, transparent communication, strong creators, and well-designed financial systems attract investors for decades. Worlds that lack direction eventually fade, and their land becomes illiquid. A platform's future vision is your roadmap for its future value.

Digital real estate valuation is not speculation—it is analysis. Once you understand scarcity, utility, location, community, tokenomics, development, cultural identity, and platform vision, you can confidently evaluate land across any metaverse world. This gives you the ability to find undervalued parcels before the masses, invest with strategy rather than emotion, and build a long-term profitable portfolio in Web3.

"The Auction House"

Marcus had always been fascinated by markets. As a kid, he collected rare sports cards. As a teenager, he flipped sneakers. As an adult, he traded stocks. But nothing prepared him for the moment he stepped into the **Neon Hall Auction House**, a glowing floating structure in The Sandbox where hundreds of avatars bid on digital land.

The hall pulsed with electric blue light. Holographic parcels rotated above the crowd like shimmering cubes, each one labeled with coordinates and details: size, district, nearby landmarks, previous sale history. The place was alive with whispers, calculations, and anticipation. Marcus stood still, absorbing everything. This wasn't a game. It was a marketplace of the future.

A robotic voice boomed overhead: "Auction Lot #742: Parcel near the Snoopverse. Opening bid: 1.8 ETH." The crowd buzzed. Marcus's instincts kicked in. He watched bidders carefully—who they were, what they valued, how confident they appeared. One avatar named *CryptoViking* immediately raised the bid. Another, a sleek neon-clad figure, matched it. Marcus looked up at the floating parcel. Located just three steps from the Snoop Dogg mansion. High traffic. High visibility. It was clear why people wanted it.

But Marcus had learned something during his research: not all value is visible. He opened a side panel showing the next few listings. One caught his attention: a parcel near an upcoming Game Maker district that hadn't yet exploded in popularity. Another was close to a new creator hub where developers met for training. Another was near a portal rumored to become a major travel point. These parcels were quieter, less glamorous—but full of hidden potential.

While the crowd battled for the celebrity-adjacent land, Marcus analyzed something else: **patterns**. The parcels that doubled in price always had one of three traits—strong utility, strong community traffic, or proximity to a future build. The most successful buyers weren't chasing hype; they were predicting momentum.

Another listing appeared: "Lot #748: Parcel near the Innovation Road expansion." The crowd barely reacted. Marcus stepped closer. He knew something they didn't. The Innovation Road district was scheduled to host a recurring weekly event by one of the biggest game creators in the metaverse. Foot traffic was guaranteed to spike.

He raised his hand. “Bid: 0.92 ETH.”

A few avatars glanced his way but didn’t respond. They were too focused on the celebrity parcel still flashing above them. Marcus smirked. He had found the undervalued treasure.

“Going once... twice... SOLD.”

The hologram flickered with a golden glow. Marcus felt a rush of adrenaline. He had just secured a parcel at a fraction of its future worth. But he wasn’t done.

He spent the next hour watching how others behaved. Some bidders only chased hype. Others followed influencers. A few quietly accumulated multiple parcels near future developments. Marcus studied them like chess masters. He understood, now more than ever, that land value wasn’t random. It was predictable. It followed patterns. It rewarded the observant.

As the auction closed, Marcus walked outside. The neon lights reflected off his avatar, painting him in bright colors. The metaverse city buzzed around him—music, movement, digital life. And for the first time, he saw it not as a game but as an ecosystem governed by the same fundamental principles he had studied his whole life.

That night, Marcus stood on his new parcel. It was empty, silent, and overlooked by everyone except him. Yet he felt the pulse of the future beneath his feet. He knew events would soon bring crowds through here. He knew creators would build next door. He knew this quiet coordinate would one day be a goldmine.

And as he gazed across the glowing skyline, Marcus realized something profound: in the metaverse, value doesn't belong to those who follow trends. It belongs to those who understand them.

Chapter 4

How to Identify High-Potential Digital Land

Identifying high-potential digital land is both an analytical process and an intuitive skill that improves with experience. In the physical world, top investors rely on data, infrastructure plans, neighborhood trends, future zoning, and local development activity. In the metaverse, the same logic applies—but with an entirely new set of variables. Digital land is not limited by geography, city ordinances, or traditional construction. Instead, its value is shaped by digital culture, community behavior, creator activity, platform roadmaps, event frequency, and the gravitational pull of digital identity. Chapter 4 teaches you the systems, tools, indicators, and psychological signals that reveal which parcels are poised for growth long before the market catches on.

The first principle of identifying high-potential land is understanding **platform momentum**. Before looking at any specific parcel, analyze whether the world itself is gaining or losing popularity. Check metrics like user growth, developer activity, event attendance, brand adoption, marketplace volume, and token performance. Are creators consistently building new experiences? Are brands hosting events? Are influencers producing content? Are roadmap updates being delivered? A parcel inside a thriving world is almost always a safer investment than a parcel in a stagnant one. This macro lens is your first line of defense against poor land decisions.

Once the platform passes the momentum test, the next factor is **map intelligence**. Every world has a unique geography, district layout, and flow of avatar traffic. Understanding how users navigate the world helps you predict which areas will grow next. Start by analyzing the macro-map: central plazas, entertainment districts, commercial zones, gaming hubs, art areas, and upcoming developments. Identify where teleportation points, portals, event venues, and primary pathways are concentrated. These areas often behave like digital versions of downtown districts in major cities—high traffic, high visibility, and high value.

The third valuation layer is **proximity analysis**. Proximity determines how often users will pass by or intentionally visit your parcel. Parcels near these hotspots almost always outperform others: – Major event venues – Portal / spawn points – Branded districts – Celebrity estates – High-utility buildings (schools, training centers, galleries) – Popular mini-games or quests – Social hubs and nightlife areas – Community hangouts – Upcoming development zones Even small parcels in these zones can appreciate rapidly if the surrounding area becomes culturally or commercially important.

The fourth component is **future development forecasting**, arguably the most profitable skill in digital real estate investing. Many investors only analyze what exists today, not what will exist in six months. The most lucrative deals usually come from buying land near districts or features that are not yet active but are planned. Study the platform's roadmap, community announcements, builder guidelines, developer streams, leaked concept art, and drafts of future features. Platforms often hint at new districts, builder tools, gameplay expansions, tournaments, festivals, and brand partnerships—long before they officially launch. If you identify these signals earlier than others, you can accumulate parcels at extremely low prices before the surge.

The fifth layer is **creator cluster analysis**. Creators are the lifeblood of digital worlds. When multiple respected builders begin constructing in a neighborhood, that area inevitably becomes culturally valuable. Creator clusters often evolve into: – entertainment districts – art villages – shopping zones – mini-game corridors – immersive event areas – education hubs Creators attract other creators, and eventually brands follow them. Buying land next to strong builders is like buying physical property next to an area where entrepreneurs and artists gather—it becomes valuable organically.

A sixth factor is **traffic pattern prediction**. While metaverse worlds evolve rapidly, user behavior follows predictable flows. Humans cluster around spectacle, community, utility, and social energy. To predict traffic, observe avatar behavior during events, new feature launches, or peak hours. Identify where crowds gather naturally and where they drift afterward. These social patterns reveal the difference between temporary hype and sustainable traffic. Land inside sustainable flow paths becomes a long-term asset.

One of the most overlooked indicators is **underpriced anomalies**, parcels priced below their true value due to oversight, inexperienced sellers, or sudden token fluctuations. Spotting these anomalies gives you instant arbitrage opportunities. Look for: – parcels priced significantly lower than neighbors – parcels with better coordinates but lower asking prices – parcels in high-traffic areas with inconsistent listing prices – owners listing multiple parcels quickly (often under value) – token dips allowing temporary discount prices Data analysis tools and map scanning help you identify these opportunities quickly.

Another powerful approach is **compositional evaluation**—examining the potential of what *could* be built, not what *is* there now. Some parcels are blank today but sit in future prime locations. Others may be adjacent to undeveloped land that will become hot districts the moment creators launch new attractions. Look for parcels that offer flexibility: easy access, ability to merge with adjacent parcels, zoning that allows multi-floor buildings, and strategic alignment with future game mechanics. These parcels can evolve from simple assets into high-value strategic holdings.

Finally, consider **long-term viability**. Not all digital worlds will survive the next decade. Not all land will remain relevant. The worlds most likely to appreciate long-term have: – strong creator ecosystems – ongoing brand partnerships – consistent user growth – deep community culture – high mobile or VR accessibility – a clear financial engine – interoperability vision – a proven track record of development Digital land is not just about buying a parcel; it is about buying into a future. High-potential land exists where technology, creativity, and community intersect. When you understand these intersections—momentum, map intelligence, proximity, future development, creator clusters, user behavior, anomalies, composition, and long-term viability—you gain a rare ability: seeing value before the world sees it.

"The Hidden District"

Lila had been wandering the metaverse for weeks, searching for a piece of land that felt right. She wasn't looking for hype or glamour—she wanted a plot with real potential. But every time she found something interesting, the price was either inflated or the location felt wrong. She had almost given up, until one rainy evening in the physical world when she stumbled across something unexpected inside Decentraland.

She teleported to the map and zoomed out. The world glowed with colored districts: entertainment, fashion, gaming, art, business. But in the lower eastern corner, she noticed a faint outline—an area with very little development, sitting between two popular districts, connected by a thin road. It was almost invisible, overshadowed by the flashy neighborhoods nearby. But something about its placement caught her eye. This zone sat exactly between a major event venue and a recently announced creator hub. It wasn't developed yet, but it was strategically positioned. Lila marked the coordinates and teleported.

The area was empty. Silent. Just a stretch of digital grass and unclaimed potential. But when she checked the map again, she noticed small clusters of builder activity forming on both sides. A well-known creator had purchased a parcel just 10 steps away. A brand had recently acquired land for an upcoming collaborative event. And the road running through the empty space was scheduled to become a major transportation route once the new teleportation update launched. Lila walked across the undeveloped land. She stood still for a moment, closing her eyes, imagining what could be here months from now: galleries, pop-up shops, interactive games, music venues, festival booths. She imagined crowds walking between the two districts, passing right through this quiet corridor. She felt the hum of future activity even though the world was empty tonight.

She opened the marketplace overlay. Only a handful of parcels were listed in this zone. One was surprisingly cheap—cheaper than parcels in worse locations. The owner had listed it without understanding what was coming. Lila's heart raced. This was exactly what she had been searching for: an undervalued gem with future potential.

"Parcel #E-193. Listed for 0.65 ETH."

She reviewed the surrounding map again. Creator clusters emerging. A brand event on the horizon. A new road connecting districts. She felt the pattern forming in front of her like a puzzle snapping into place.

Lila clicked "Buy." The confirmation flashed across her screen. She owned the first parcel in what she now believed would become one of the most important corridors in the eastern district.

Days passed. Weeks. Suddenly the creator hub opened, and foot traffic surged in the area. Builders announced new projects. A music festival organizer purchased land two parcels away. A gaming team bought a whole cluster nearby. Lila watched everything unfold like a time-lapse movie—empty fields slowly transforming into a vibrant digital neighborhood.

One evening, she stood on her parcel as avatars passed by. A creator stopped beside her and said, "You picked the right spot. This whole zone is about to explode." Lila smiled. She hadn't relied on luck—she had relied on observation, pattern recognition, and the ability to see value where others saw nothing.

The district that once felt hidden was now alive with color and motion. And her small, humble parcel—the one most people overlooked—had become one of the most sought-after pieces of land in the corridor. As she gazed across the bustling landscape, Lila realized something powerful: in the metaverse, value doesn't always exist where things *are*—it exists where things *will be*. And she had gotten there first.

Chapter 5

Flipping Digital Land: The Complete Strategy Blueprint

Flipping digital land is one of the fastest and most accessible ways to generate profit in the metaverse, especially for beginners who may not yet have the skills or resources to build large-scale experiences or rental operations. Just like physical real estate flippers, successful digital land flippers rely on timing, market psychology, opportunity identification, and rapid execution. But the metaverse adds new mechanics—token fluctuations, creator-driven value spikes, brand partnerships, gamified events, scarcity cycles, and cultural momentum. Understanding these mechanics enables you to flip parcels for maximum profit with minimal risk. In this chapter, you will learn the full flipping blueprint: how to find undervalued parcels, how to evaluate flip potential, when to buy, when to hold, when to sell, and how to generate consistent returns month after month.

The first principle of profitable flipping is **understanding market cycles**. Metaverse land markets move in waves shaped by platform updates, token price trends, news events, influencer activity, and brand announcements. These cycles include accumulation periods (low price, low hype), build-up periods (increasing interest), hype waves (high demand and fast sales), and correction phases (price normalization). The best flips occur when you buy during accumulation or build-up phases and sell during hype waves. Timing a flip is not about predicting the exact top—it is about recognizing when demand surges faster than supply. Smart flippers don't try to catch the highest peak; they catch the safest, most profitable middle.

The second pillar is **identifying undervalued parcels** using data-driven criteria. Undervalued parcels usually fall into several categories: those listed by inexperienced sellers who don't understand true value; those located in areas about to receive a district expansion, event, or new creator activity; those priced lower because of temporary token dips; those mispriced relative to neighboring parcels; those owned by bulk holders liquidating several plots quickly; and parcels in areas that have future rather than present value. A flipper's goal is to buy where value will soon emerge, not where it already exists. You profit from trends others haven't seen yet.

A third essential flipping skill is **rapid market scanning**, using both official maps and third-party tools to detect price anomalies. Scan for parcels listed 10–40% lower than surrounding plots. Look for new listings posted within the last hour. Look for sellers dropping prices repeatedly to liquidate quickly. Look for plots adjacent to new builds, event venues, or branded attractions. Look for parcels with low asking prices but high traffic potential. Flippers succeed because they spot opportunities in minutes—not days.

Next is **evaluating flip potential**, which requires assessing the immediate catalysts that could raise parcel value. Catalysts include: – new district openings – large events approaching – brand announcements – influencer partnerships – builder competitions – token rallies – upcoming updates that increase traffic or utility – creator migrations into specific neighborhoods – economic shifts inside the platform If a catalyst is coming within the next few weeks, a flip becomes significantly easier and more profitable.

An often overlooked but incredibly powerful flipping method is **pre-event flipping**. Before major festivals, brand activations, metaverse conferences, or platform-wide events, land prices in nearby districts rise dramatically. Months before Decentraland's annual Metaverse Fashion Week, savvy flippers buy land near runways, plazas, and fashion districts. When The Sandbox announces game maker competitions, flippers target parcels near creator hubs. Buying before these surges allows for fast flips as the event date approaches and demand spikes.

Another technique is **flipping through repositioning**, where the asset itself remains the same, but the listing presentation changes. Many sellers list land without descriptions, photos, or contextual details. When flippers purchase these parcels, they improve the listing by adding district benefits, nearby attractions, future development insights, and premium keywords. This simple repositioning often adds 10–30% value even before market-driven appreciation kicks in. In the metaverse, marketing the parcel is part of the flipping strategy.

A highly effective approach for mid-range investors is **cluster flipping**. Instead of flipping one parcel at a time, flippers purchase 2–5 undervalued parcels in a zone predicted to appreciate. When the area gains momentum, they flip the parcels strategically—selling one early to recover the initial investment, another at mid-appreciation, and saving one for the peak. This creates a self-funding flipping cycle with reduced risk.

For advanced flippers, **merge flipping** offers high returns. Some worlds allow parcels to be merged into estates. Two low-value parcels, when combined, become a single high-value estate that attracts brands, builders, and creators. The merged estate sells for significantly more than the combined cost of individual parcels. This tactic requires capital but yields powerful returns in bullish markets. Timing the sale is as important as timing the purchase. Effective flippers watch demand indicators closely: increasing listing views, fast sales in the neighborhood, token price momentum, social media hype, new creator activity, and rising trade volume. When these indicators accelerate together, the market is entering a seller's window. The goal is not to be greedy—the goal is to exit with profit before correction cycles arrive.

Finally, all flippers must master **risk management**. Avoid flipping in worlds with declining user activity, unclear roadmaps, or unstable tokenomics. Always diversify across different districts or worlds. Never put all capital into hype-driven parcels without underlying utility. Keep a percentage of capital liquid so you can jump on unexpected opportunities. And most importantly, treat flipping as a business—not a gamble. When done correctly, flipping digital land is a systematic, predictable, and scalable income strategy in Web3.

"The 48-Hour Flip"

Jonas wasn't a gambler. He liked calculated risks—moves that rewarded intelligence, not luck. When he first entered The Sandbox, he didn't buy land immediately. He studied the map for weeks, watched auctions, followed creators, analyzed price charts, and observed user behavior. He wanted his first flip to be strategic, not impulsive. And one night, the perfect opportunity appeared. It happened while he was casually scanning the marketplace. A small parcel near the Game Maker Academy district was listed far below surrounding prices. At first, he thought it was a glitch. Then he checked the seller's profile. They were offloading multiple parcels that night—clearly someone liquidating fast. Jonas clicked the listing details: "Parcel #GMA-114. Asking price: 0.75 ETH." The lowest parcel near that district had recently sold for 1.4 ETH. Jonas's pulse quickened. This wasn't just underpriced—it was a steal.

But he didn't rush. He zoomed out on the map and noticed something interesting: the Game Maker Academy was hosting a major creator competition in 10 days. Thousands of creators would flood this district during the event. Foot traffic would surge. Demand would spike. And land prices would almost certainly rise.

He looked again at the listing. Still available. Still unbelievably cheap. Jonas whispered to himself, "This is it." He clicked "Buy." The screen flashed green. The parcel was his.

Rather than listing it immediately, Jonas decided to reposition it. He opened a fresh listing window and began crafting a compelling description:

"Prime parcel near the Game Maker Academy. High creator traffic. Perfect for interactive builds, mini-games, galleries, or event pop-ups. Major competition coming soon. Rare opportunity."

He added screenshots, marked nearby attractions, and highlighted the upcoming event. Then he waited.

Within hours, the listing began receiving views. By the next morning, offers came in—small ones at first. But Jonas held firm. He knew what was coming. As the event date approached, creators began swarming the district. The marketplace lit up with activity. Prices climbed rapidly.

On the second evening, just 36 hours after he purchased the parcel, a message popped up: "Offer received: 1.35 ETH." Jonas leaned back in his chair, smiling. That was almost double what he paid. But he sensed there was still room to grow. He countered with 1.55 ETH. The buyer accepted instantly.

The flip was done. Jonas stared at his screen, stunned. He had just made more profit in 48 hours than he made in a week at his full-time job.

He could've stopped there, satisfied. But something about the experience awakened a fire in him. This wasn't luck—it was strategy. Observation, timing, data, and patience. Jonas returned to the map, scanning for the next opportunity. Soon, he spotted another undervalued parcel near an emerging creator hub. And another near a district rumored to host branded events. The flips kept coming. Some took days. Others took weeks. But each one sharpened his instincts. Jonas transformed from a curious newcomer into one of the sharpest flippers in the district. People began messaging him for tips, market insights, and prediction charts. They didn't know he wasn't guessing—he was reading patterns others ignored.

Months later, Jonas stood on the balcony of a parcel he had bought early and held long-term. Below him, avatars walked through a lively corridor of mini-games, galleries, shops, and studios. The area had blossomed into one of the most active districts in the world. And he had seen it long before anyone else.

Jonas realized something important that night: flipping wasn't about chasing hype. It was about seeing value before the world woke up. It was about timing, discipline, and vision. And in the metaverse, vision was the most valuable currency of all.

Chapter 6

Renting Digital Land & Creating Passive Income

Renting digital land is one of the most powerful, reliable, and scalable ways to generate passive income in the metaverse. Unlike flipping—which requires timing, fast decisions, and active involvement—renting transforms digital land into a long-term cash-producing asset that can pay you month after month. As more creators, brands, educators, artists, and entertainers enter the metaverse, demand for temporary access to prime digital locations continues to grow. But to rent land profitably, you must understand the mechanics of digital leasing, tenant demand patterns, pricing strategies, rental risk management, and the tools used to automate rental operations. Chapter 6 breaks down every element of digital land renting so you can build a predictable income engine from your virtual properties.

The foundation of digital renting begins with **understanding who the tenants are**. Unlike physical real estate, metaverse tenants aren't families or long-term occupants—they are creators, builders, event organizers, brands, game developers, gallery owners, musicians, influencers, educators, and business owners. Each tenant type has unique needs. Some require only a few days of access to host a pop-up concert, art exhibition, or workshop. Others need weeks or months to develop a game, build a store, or run a recurring event. The key to maximizing rental demand is targeting tenant categories your parcel naturally attracts. Land near event venues attracts organizers. Land near creator hubs attracts developers. Land near galleries attracts artists, and land near fashion districts attracts designers and advertisers.

Next, you must understand **utility-based demand**, which is the primary driver of rental value. Tenants choose parcels based on visibility, traffic, convenience, district alignment, and development potential. Parcels near plazas, portals, festivals, brand districts, or major creator zones command higher rent. But even less central parcels can achieve strong demand if they are located near useful features like roads, transport hubs, or upcoming development. The more valuable the location for a tenant's mission, the higher the rent you can charge.

The third component is **pricing strategy**. Digital land renting operates in flexible timeframes—daily, weekly, monthly, seasonal, or event-based rentals. Short-term rentals typically yield higher returns per day but require more management or automation. Long-term rentals offer consistent income and lower management effort but lower daily revenue. Optimal pricing depends on market volatility, platform popularity, and tenant availability. During major events like Metaverse Fashion Week or large gaming tournaments, short-term rental prices can spike dramatically. When platforms are in quieter phases, longer-term leases stabilize income. Smart landlords balance both: rent short during event seasons, secure longer tenants during slow cycles.

A fourth key principle is **smart contract leasing**, which is the backbone of digital rental transactions. In decentralized worlds, most rental agreements occur through platforms where smart contracts manage access rights. These contracts automatically grant temporary building permissions while protecting land ownership. They also ensure transparent payment, automated expiration, and non-renewal unless both parties agree. Understanding smart contract terms—permissions, expiration, rights, and renewal rules—is essential to avoid disputes or unintended access.

Another important aspect is **property development before renting**. Empty land often rents for less than developed land. Simple structures like stages, galleries, shops, or event-ready platforms can dramatically increase rental value. Even pre-built modular spaces, such as drag-and-drop structures or customizable rooms, attract tenants seeking quick setup. A strategic landlord invests in lightweight builds that make the parcel more appealing while maintaining flexibility. Think of it like furnishing an apartment—furnished units often rent faster and at higher rates.

A sixth factor is **building niche-specific rental properties**, which is a secret advantage that experienced digital landlords use to dominate the market. The concept is simple: create spaces tailored to specific industries. Build a gallery for artists, a conference room for educators, an arena for gamers, a runway for designers, a lounge for influencers, or a shop for creators. These specialized spaces attract reliable tenant categories who are willing to pay premium rates for convenience and functionality. The more tailored the build, the stronger the demand.

Risk management is another essential skill. The metaverse is highly dynamic, and rental demand can fluctuate. To mitigate risk, landlords must diversify across platforms, districts, tenant types, and rental durations. Instead of relying on one parcel or one tenant category, landlords build small portfolios across several high-demand zones. They also avoid relying solely on event-based activity. Sustainable rental income comes from serving creators who build, teach, entertain, and host experiences year-round.

Automation plays a critical role in scaling rental operations. Many decentralized worlds offer rental smart contract platforms that streamline listing, leasing, payments, permissions, renewals, and expirations. Automated systems allow landlords to manage multiple parcels without daily manual work. Tools also track rental analytics, visitor metrics, and pricing adjustments to ensure optimized income. In high-performing portfolios, automation eliminates 80–90% of the workload, allowing landlords to grow without burnout.

One of the most profitable strategies is **seasonal arbitrage**, which involves renting parcels specifically during demand spikes, then holding or developing them during slow periods. For example, renting land during a fashion event cycle, then building a small attraction afterward for steady income. Or renting parcels during a gaming tournament, then holding them until the next major creator event. Seasonal timing allows landlords to maximize returns while reducing vacancy risk.

Finally, the long-term vision of digital renting is enormous. As the metaverse expands, digital tenants will not just be brands and creators—they will be AI agents, automated businesses, autonomous stores, and persistent experiences powered by smart NPCs. Digital renting will evolve from short-term creative leases into an entire economy of AI-powered businesses renting digital space for 24/7 operation. Understanding rental strategy today positions you to dominate a future where passive income is not just profitable—it is automated at scale.

"The Tenant From Nowhere"

Ariana never planned to become a digital landlord. She bought her first parcel in Decentraland because she loved the neon skyline and wanted a small place to experiment with builds. But one night, everything changed.

She was standing on her parcel—a modest but well-located piece of land near a teleportation hub—when a message popped up.

"Hi. Are you renting this land?"

Ariana blinked. She wasn't. She hadn't even considered it. But curiosity nudged her to reply.

"Maybe. What do you need?"

The avatar introduced himself as Rune, a creator building a rapid-fire interactive concert series. He needed land for only four days to test an experimental show that blended holograms, sound tunnels, and AI-generated music. He didn't want to buy land—he needed something temporary.

Ariana hesitated. "I've never rented land before."

Rune laughed. "It's easy. I can handle the setup." They negotiated a short-term contract. He offered 0.25 ETH upfront. Ariana felt a spark of excitement—this was more than she expected for such a short duration. She initiated a smart contract, double-checked permissions, and granted temporary building access.

Within two hours, Rune transformed the empty parcel into a glowing performance space. The stage pulsed with shifting geometric patterns. AI-driven musical waves rippled across the sky. By nightfall, avatars crowded the space, dancing, taking screenshots, streaming live videos, and tagging her land.

Ariana watched the chaos unfold—awed, speechless, exhilarated. She wasn't a developer, musician, or performer, yet her land was the stage for something extraordinary.

After Rune's event concluded, he messaged her again. "Your land has great traffic. You should definitely rent."

And then, more messages came. Artists. Educators. A small brand wanting a pop-up shop. A fashion creator planning a holographic runway. All asking the same question:

"Is your parcel available for rent?"

Ariana quickly adapted. She built a simple modular event space—a glowing dome with movable walls and customizable lighting. Suddenly, renting became effortless. Tenants loved the plug-and-play setup. Weeks later, a music label reached out, offering a long-term lease. She negotiated a monthly rate. Then another tenant wanted a weekly rental. Ariana divided her land into time blocks, scheduling events like a hotel booking system.

Her wallet grew. Her land's reputation grew. Her confidence grew.

The breakthrough came when she built a second space—a sleek gallery designed specifically for NFT artists. Within days, the gallery was fully booked. Some creators rented space monthly. Others booked for weekend exhibitions.

Ariana could barely believe it. She wasn't flipping parcels. She wasn't designing complex games. She was simply renting space—yet she was earning more from digital tenants than from her physical-world contract job.

One evening, while reviewing rental analytics, she teleported to her parcel. A gentle breeze swept across the digital grass. Her event dome glowed softly in the distance. She heard music from a live performance happening inside. Avatars gathered around, laughing, dancing, connecting.

A quiet realization settled over her: her land wasn't just property. It was opportunity—alive, dynamic, and filled with people who wanted to build something.

A tenant from nowhere had turned her into a landlord. And now, the metaverse itself was her neighborhood.

Chapter 7

Developing Digital Property: Building Experiences, Businesses, and Value

Developing digital property is where digital real estate transforms from static land into a dynamic asset capable of generating significant financial, cultural, and community value. In physical real estate, development is expensive and slow. In the metaverse, development is creative, flexible, customizable, and often instantaneous. Building experiences, shops, games, galleries, classrooms, lounges, or entire entertainment zones on your digital land increases its usefulness, visibility, and revenue potential. The more valuable and interactive your development is, the more the parcel itself appreciates. Chapter 7 provides a complete blueprint for transforming raw digital land into a high-performing, high-value digital property that attracts users, tenants, brands, and long-term wealth.

The first principle of effective digital development is **purpose alignment**. Before building anything, you must understand what purpose your parcel will serve. Is the goal to attract tenants? Host events? Generate traffic? Sell products? Showcase art? Provide education? Run a game? Build a brand presence? A parcel without a purpose becomes a random build that nobody uses. But a parcel with a focused purpose becomes a destination. Your development should align with the strengths of your district. Build galleries in art zones, shops in commercial zones, event spaces in high-traffic plazas, and games near entertainment districts. Purpose alignment ensures your development has built-in demand.

The second principle is **experiential design**, the cornerstone of successful metaverse builds. Unlike physical property, digital environments are not limited by gravity, materials, or physics. You can build floating structures, interactive tunnels, holographic stages, moving platforms, animated sculptures, sound-reactive walls, or AI-powered NPCs. Users are drawn to novelty, interactivity, and immersion. Experiences that feel alive—pulsing lights, reactive music, customizable environments—attract visitors repeatedly. The more memorable your development is, the more it becomes a magnet for creators and communities.

A third essential factor is **accessibility and flow**, which influence user behavior and engagement. Good development is not just beautiful—it is intuitive. Make entrances easy to find, spawn points clear, pathways obvious, and interactions simple. Avoid clutter or overly complex designs that confuse users. Structure your build so visitors naturally move from one area to the next, discovering more as they explore. Add intuitive signage, guided pathways, and spatial organization. A well-designed flow leads to longer stay times, more event participation, and stronger word-of-mouth visibility.

Another powerful development concept is **modular architecture**—building structures that can be easily modified, re-themed, or repurposed without tearing everything down. Modular builds allow you to adapt quickly to changing trends, tenant needs, seasonal events, or new platform tools. For example, a modular gallery can become a classroom, a pop-up store, or a social lounge with minimal redesign. A modular stage can shift themes for different performers. Modular architecture saves time, protects your investment, and allows you to scale.

A fifth major development strategy is **interactive functionality**, which is a unique advantage digital real estate has over physical real estate. Interactivity can include mini-games, teleportation pads, loot drops, quests, educational modules, interactive panels, dynamic lighting, sound zones, or user-triggered animations. Interactive experiences increase user retention dramatically and create repeat visitors. They also appeal to brands, creators, and event organizers who need engaging environments for their content. Interactivity is not optional—it is a core driver of digital value.

Next, consider **brand collaboration potential**, one of the most lucrative aspects of digital development. Brands entering the metaverse often seek developed spaces rather than blank land. They want ready-to-use galleries, event halls, theaters, classrooms, or themed environments. Well-developed properties become premium rental spaces or partnership assets. Building branded-friendly spaces increases your land's commercial potential. Even small builds like minimalist galleries or sleek presentation stages can attract partnerships from small businesses, startups, or content creators.

A seventh ingredient of valuable development is **optimization and performance**. While creativity is limitless, performance is not. Builds must load quickly, run smoothly, and be accessible across devices. Overly heavy builds reduce traffic because users avoid lag. Optimization includes reducing unnecessary animations, optimizing textures, controlling sound layers, minimizing excessive scripts, and testing across devices. A smooth experience increases visitor retention and ensures your property is viable long-term as platforms evolve.

Another critical factor is **community integration**. A developed property becomes valuable when it becomes part of the surrounding community. Attend builder meetups, collaborate with creators, host open gallery nights, sponsor small events, or open your space for community use. Becoming a community hub increases both land visibility and district value. Communities reward owners who enhance the neighborhood, and platform ecosystems prioritize builds that drive active engagement.

One of the highest-value development strategies is **multi-purpose design**—building environments that serve more than one function. For example: – A gallery + event venue – A store + training center – A lounge + rentable meeting room – A mini-game + NFT shop – A classroom + networking hub Multi-purpose spaces ensure your property stays relevant across platforms, events, seasons, and market cycles.

Finally, long-term development requires **vision**, not just builds. The most successful digital property developers look ahead—anticipating future platform updates, technological shifts, cultural trends, and new monetization models. They build adaptable properties that can evolve with the metaverse. Digital development is not about building what exists today; it is about building what the future will demand. When your parcel aligns with future needs—immersive entertainment, AI-generated content, creator collaboration, virtual education, social identity, or interactive commerce—it becomes an appreciating asset and a cornerstone of long-term digital wealth.

"The Build That Changed Everything"

When Maya bought her digital parcel in The Sandbox, it was nothing more than a small cube of empty land floating in a bright pixelated world. She didn't know how to build. She didn't know how to script. She didn't even know what she wanted the parcel to be. All she knew was that she wanted to create something that felt alive—something that made people stop, look, and say, "Wow."

For weeks, she explored the world, visiting galleries, games, stores, lounges, and event venues. She watched how avatars moved, where they gathered, and what kind of environments they stayed in the longest. She noticed that people didn't just want beautiful spaces—they wanted interactive spaces. Places where something happened. Places where the environment responded to them. Places where they felt part of the story.

One evening, while watching a creator workshop, inspiration struck her like lightning: she would build a place that reacted to movement, sound, and presence. A space that shifted based on its visitors. A digital sanctuary of light.

She started small. A floating platform. A few pillars. A glowing floor. Then she added interactive lights—panels that flickered when avatars stepped on them. She added music that pulsed whenever someone entered. She added walls that shifted colors as users walked by.

Days later, she added more: – a sound tunnel that amplified footsteps into soft harmonies – a floating crystal garden that glowed when approached – a sky that changed based on avatar movement – holographic sculptures that rotated on voice activation

Her parcel became a living canvas.

Soon, avatars wandered in—first curious explorers, then creators, then influencers. They streamed videos, posted screenshots, and shared clips. Visitors described it as “the light temple,” “the responsive sanctuary,” and “the world that listens.” The name stuck.

One day, Maya received a message from a small but growing virtual fashion brand.

“We love your space. Can we host a show here?”

Maya’s heart pounded. She had never imagined brands taking notice. She agreed. The show brought hundreds of avatars. Influencers filmed the runway. The brand paid her generously for the event rental. Afterward, an artist reached out: **“Can I**

use your sanctuary for my exhibition?" Then a game developer sent a proposal: **"Can we collaborate on a performance hall based on your design?"**

The sanctuary became more than a build. It became a phenomenon. A place that lived and breathed through its visitors. A place that made people feel something.

But the true turning point came weeks later when a major metaverse entertainment company contacted her.

"Your sanctuary aligns perfectly with our new immersive event series. We'd like to partner on long-term installations. Are you available for a call?"

Maya sat still for a long moment. She had started with no plan, no experience, no expectations. She just wanted to build something meaningful. Now brands, artists, developers, and influencers were lining up to collaborate.

She teleported to the sanctuary that night. The sky shifted from violet to golden as she arrived, reacting to her presence. The lights shimmered beneath her feet. The air hummed softly. It felt alive, just as she dreamed.

She whispered to herself, "I built this."

And in that moment, she understood something profound: in the metaverse, development was not limited by skill or background—it was limited only by imagination. Digital land was a blank canvas, and anyone with vision could turn it into something extraordinary.

Her sanctuary was no longer just a build. It was a destination. A business. A landmark. A story written in light.

And it all began with a single empty plot of digital soil.

Chapter 8

Marketing, Traffic, and Visibility: How to Attract Users to Your Digital Property

Building or buying digital land is only half the equation; the other half is making sure people actually visit it. In the metaverse, visibility is the currency that converts a static property into a thriving experience. Whether your goal is to rent your land, flip it, host events, build a business, sell NFTs, or increase long-term property value, you must understand how traffic works and how to drive it with intention. Visibility amplifies everything. A parcel seen by thousands becomes more valuable than one hidden in a quiet corner, even if they share identical coordinates. Chapter 8 teaches you the complete traffic blueprint: how to market your land, attract visitors, collaborate with other creators, leverage community culture, and turn your property into a well-known destination.

The first pillar of digital visibility is **platform-native discovery**. Every metaverse world has built-in discovery systems—maps, trending listings, featured experiences, recommended builds, event boards, creator hubs, or teleport portals. When your parcel is optimized for these systems, you organically attract visitors without paying for promotion. Add clear descriptions, tags, high-quality thumbnails, and consistent updates so your parcel is recognized by platform algorithms as active and relevant. Worlds reward activity. Parcels that sit idle rarely get featured. Parcels that update frequently—new events, new art, new features—often rise in visibility.

The second key factor is **event-driven traffic**, one of the fastest ways to generate large visitor spikes. Events include live performances, workshops, exhibitions, game tournaments, networking meetups, product launches, festivals, and creator reveals. Even small events can generate significant traffic if promoted properly. Hosting recurring weekly events—like "Creator Friday," "Music Night," or "NFT Spotlight"—creates habit-based traffic where users return repeatedly because they know something is happening. Event-driven traffic also increases long-term property value because parcels with active histories attract more tenants and buyers.

A third major visibility driver is **cross-platform marketing**. The metaverse doesn't exist in isolation; it thrives through external channels like YouTube, TikTok, Instagram, Discord, X, and streaming platforms. Recording walkthroughs, posting screenshots, streaming live events, sharing behind-the-scenes build videos, and collaborating with influencers dramatically expand your property's reach. Many parcels become popular simply because they appear in viral videos or trending creator clips. You don't need to be an influencer yourself—you only need to partner with those who already have an audience.

The fourth component is **community integration**, which is crucial in Web3 ecosystems. Communities drive attention, value, culture, and relevance. Joining creator groups, DAO channels, district communities, art collectives, or event groups helps you get organic promotion through community calendars, newsletters, or collaborative events. Communities amplify each other. When your property becomes associated with a respected group—like a major art collective or popular gaming crew—its visibility multiplies.

Next, consider **collaboration-based visibility**, one of the most powerful marketing strategies in the metaverse. Collaboration might involve co-hosting an event, building a shared experience, offering your space to creators for free in exchange for exposure, or creating multi-parcel attractions with neighbors. In digital worlds, collaboration spreads brand presence exponentially because every creator brings their own audience. A small parcel can gain massive visibility simply by partnering with a well-known builder, musician, or NFT artist.

A sixth strategy is **experience-driven virality**, where the design itself causes users to share the space. Interactive builds—like jumping puzzles, AI-driven environments, photogenic scenes, creative illusions, or unexpected surprises—motivate users to share content. Viral builds often require good design, but they also benefit from psychological triggers: novelty, challenge, beauty, humor, or emotional resonance. When a space feels magical or unique, visitors naturally invite others.

Another major factor in visibility is **search engine indexing**. Yes, metaverse properties can appear on Google. By creating articles, pages, or posts featuring your parcel name, district location, event schedule, or project branding, you increase discoverability across the broader internet. This is especially useful for galleries, educational centers, showrooms, or branded attractions. When people search for "Decentraland gallery" or "Sandbox event venue," your property can appear in search results if optimized correctly.

A seventh element is **building recognizable identity and branding**. Brands aren't just for companies—personal brands thrive in the metaverse too. Give your property a name, theme, color palette, logo, and consistent story. Famous metaverse destinations often become iconic because they feel coherent and memorable. Whether you build a cyberpunk lounge, floating temple, creator dojo, or AI-powered gallery, a unique identity helps visitors remember and return. Eighth is **traffic loop engineering**, meaning the deliberate design of experiences that encourage movement, exploration, and return visits. Create pathways that lead users to different attractions. Add teleport points, reward zones, or hidden rooms. Build quests with daily tasks, collectible items, or rotating content. Use notifications, Discord posts, or announcements to encourage recurring participation. The more reasons people have to return, the higher your long-term visibility becomes.

The ninth visibility strategy is **rental-based traffic leverage**. Renting your land to creators, brands, or performers increases traffic automatically because they bring their own audience. Some digital landlords focus solely on this model—allowing tenants to generate visibility for them. After multiple tenants use the same property, the parcel becomes known as an active space, increasing its reputation and rental price.

Finally, the most powerful and sustainable visibility factor is **cultural relevance**. In the metaverse, culture is everything. People gather around creativity, identity, humor, art, music, gaming, and shared meaning. If your property contributes to culture—through events, builds, storytelling, community collaborations, or creator participation—it becomes part of the world's fabric. Cultural destinations appreciate over time, draw visitors organically, and remain relevant even as trends shift. When you build for culture, you build for longevity.

Marketing in the metaverse is not about advertising—it is about creating gravity. When your property has purpose, identity, interactivity, community presence, and collaborative energy, it becomes a magnet that attracts visitors naturally. With consistent effort, your digital land transforms from a quiet plot into a living, breathing attraction seen and loved by thousands.

"The Day the World Found Her Gallery"

Elara's gallery was her secret. She built it quietly over several months—a glowing, crystalline structure on a modest parcel in an art district of Decentraland. It floated gently above the ground, its walls shimmering like ice under neon skies. Inside, holographic paintings rotated slowly, each one handcrafted with care. She never advertised it. She never posted it. She believed that if the art was good enough, people would eventually find it.

But they didn't.

Days passed. Then weeks. Then months. Visitors came rarely—maybe three or four a week, mostly explorers who stumbled in by accident. Elara was proud of her work but frustrated by its invisibility. She wondered if she wasn't skilled enough, or if the metaverse was simply too big for quiet creations to be seen.

One night, she sat alone inside the gallery, watching holographic colors dance across empty floors. She whispered to herself, “Maybe I need to help the world find it.” The next morning, she launched a tiny experiment.

She messaged a small NFT art collective: **“Would any of your artists like to host a one-day exhibition in my gallery? Free of charge.”**

Within hours, she received three enthusiastic replies.

The collective posted the event in their Discord. A micro-influencer tweeted about it. A creator added the location to a community calendar.

On the night of the exhibition, Elara watched in disbelief as the gallery filled with avatars—first a few, then dozens, then over a hundred. They took photos, posted videos, complimented the space, and asked when the next event would be.

Her gallery wasn’t a secret anymore.

Inspired, Elara started hosting monthly exhibitions. Then weekly showcases. She collaborated with musicians, poets, wearable designers, and VR sculptors. One creator asked if he could record a livestream inside the gallery. Another asked if she could rent out the space for a fashion drop.

Each collaboration brought a new wave of visitors.

Still, the breakthrough arrived unexpectedly. A famous metaverse streamer known for reviewing digital worlds visited during a random Wednesday showcase. He walked through the gallery, pausing in awe at the crystalline walls. He panned his camera up, capturing floating artwork refracting through digital prisms.

"This," he said to thousands watching live, "is one of the most beautiful hidden spaces in Decentraland."

The clip went viral overnight.

Within a day, hundreds of visitors swarmed her gallery. Within a week, thousands. People teleported from across the metaverse just to see the "Crystal Sanctuary." They posted videos, wrote articles, and shared screenshots. Her parcel appeared on the trending map. Her gallery became a landmark.

But the moment that meant the most came later that month, when a new visitor approached her.

"Are you Elara?" the avatar asked.

"Yes."

"I just wanted to say... your gallery inspired me to build my first world. Thank you."

Elara felt her chest tighten. For the first time, she realized visibility wasn't about fame—it was about impact. Her work mattered because it reached people. Because it made them feel something. Because it inspired them to create.

That night, she teleported back to her gallery. Visitors roamed happily, talking, laughing, photographing. The walls glowed in warm hues. Her art sparkled like living gems.

She whispered again—only this time with pride:

"The world found it."

And she knew, deep in her heart, that this was just the beginning.

Chapter 9

Evaluating Risks, Scams, and Market Volatility in Digital Real Estate

Every opportunity—especially one as new and fast-moving as digital real estate—comes with risk. The metaverse is a powerful economic frontier filled with early adopters, creators, brands, and visionaries, but it also attracts poorly run projects, abandoned worlds, inflated markets, fake land schemes, unofficial sellers, unstable tokens, and hype-driven bubbles. Understanding risk is not meant to scare you away from investing; it is meant to make you a more strategic, confident, and profitable investor who can navigate the digital world with clarity rather than emotion. Chapter 9 gives you a comprehensive framework for evaluating risks, spotting scams, recognizing market traps, protecting your assets, and building a long-term strategy that survives volatility.

The first risk category is **platform risk**, which measures the stability, growth, and long-term viability of the metaverse world itself. Many worlds emerge quickly and disappear just as fast. A platform without consistent users, development updates, clear leadership, funding, brand partnerships, or creator adoption presents significant long-term risk. Before investing in any land parcel, evaluate whether the world has strong technological foundations, engaged communities, a roadmap it actually follows, a functioning marketplace, and active builders. Land inside a thriving world appreciates. Land inside a declining world becomes illiquid. Platform health is the backbone of all digital land value.

The second category is **economic risk**, which includes token volatility, inflation, liquidity issues, and market manipulation. Because most digital land transactions depend on platform tokens (like MANA, SAND, APE, or native coins of emerging worlds), token swings impact land price dramatically. A token crash can temporarily erase 20–40% of land value even if demand remains strong. Conversely, token spikes can artificially inflate land prices without true value growth. Investors must separate land value from token performance by evaluating demand, traffic, development, and community behavior independently. Token momentum should inform decisions—not dictate them.

Next is **speculation risk**, one of the most common pitfalls. Many new investors buy land based on hype cycles, influencer announcements, viral videos, or trending news rather than analysis. Hype-driven land purchases often occur at price peaks, leading to long-term losses when the hype fades. Avoid speculation by purchasing based on map intelligence, district analysis, platform adoption, and future development—not emotions. Smart investors buy when the market is quiet and sell when the world is loud, not the other way around.

A fourth major risk is **scam risk**, which includes fake land listings, unofficial marketplaces, phishing attacks, contract impersonations, and fraudulent sellers. Because all legitimate digital land exists as verifiable NFTs on-chain, every transaction must occur through official or trusted marketplaces. Scammers often create fake websites, misleading login pages, or counterfeit listings. Investors must double-check URLs, verify contract addresses, only connect wallets on official domains, and never click links received through private messages. Scams grow during hype waves; discipline protects you.

Another critical category is **liquidity risk**, meaning how easily you can sell your land. Even good platforms experience slow periods where buying activity drops. Some land parcels—especially those far from districts or within low-demand areas—may take longer to sell. Liquidity depends on parcel desirability, platform popularity, overall sentiment, and timing. To reduce liquidity risk, invest in high-traffic areas, near creator hubs, along teleportation routes, or inside popular districts. These areas retain liquidity even during slower cycles.

The sixth risk category is **development risk**, which refers to the uncertainty of platform updates. Some worlds promise advanced tools, interactivity, new districts, VR integration, or builder upgrades that take longer than expected—or never arrive. Delays can temporarily stall land appreciation. Lack of delivery can damage trust. Investors must assess whether the development team has a history of executing updates on time, communicating openly, and delivering meaningful improvements. A world with slow development may still succeed—but expectations must match reality.

Government and regulatory risk is another emerging category. While digital land itself does not fall under traditional real estate law, blockchain transactions and token-based economies may face increasing regulation over time. This could influence taxation, reporting requirements, or marketplace operations. Investors should stay informed on global Web3 regulation trends, especially in the U.S., EU, and Asia, but should not allow fear to overshadow opportunity. Regulation often stabilizes markets rather than destroying them.

Another overlooked category is **technology risk**, especially regarding wallets, security practices, and user behavior. Investors must secure their assets through hardware wallets, strong passwords, multi-factor authentication, and phishing awareness. A hacked wallet can lead to irreversible loss. Understanding wallet security, private key protection, and safe browsing practices is essential. In digital real estate, your wallet is your title deed. Protect it like your most valuable asset.

Then there is **market cycle risk**, tied to broader crypto cycles. During bear markets, land prices typically dip as token prices fall and fewer users spend heavily. During bull markets, speculation increases. Investors who ignore cycles often misinterpret temporary price declines as permanent failures or temporary price rises as guaranteed success. The key is understanding that digital land follows long-term adoption curves, not short-term hype spikes. Long-term investors accumulate during down cycles and enjoy massive appreciation during platform growth phases. Short-term investors must time exits carefully to avoid corrections.

Finally, **personal risk tolerance** must be measured. Digital real estate is exciting, but it requires patience, analysis, emotional stability, and strategic thinking. Investors should never risk capital they cannot afford to hold long-term. Success in this space comes from calculated decisions, diversified strategies, strong research, community involvement, and continuous adaptation. Risk cannot be eliminated—but it can be mastered. And when mastered, it transforms digital real estate from a gamble into a powerful and sustainable wealth-building engine.

"The Parcel That Almost Destroyed Him"

Riven had always been bold. Some called him fearless. Others called him reckless. In the early days of his metaverse journey, he thought courage alone would carry him through any investment. But nothing prepared him for the day he bought the parcel that almost destroyed him.

It happened during a hype cycle unlike anything he'd seen before. A new world—LumaVerse—had launched with breathtaking trailers, celebrity endorsements, and promises of a revolutionary builder engine. Social media was buzzing. Influencers shouted about "once-in-a-lifetime land drops." Prices were rising hourly. Everyone seemed certain it would become the next big metaverse.

Riven jumped in without thinking.

He bought a parcel at the peak—four times the price of early listings—believing it would double again within days. His friends warned him to slow down, but he couldn't hear them. Hype drowned out reason. Excitement blurred caution. He felt unstoppable.

For a week, everything looked perfect. Announcements flowed daily. The community Discord grew to hundreds of thousands. People flipped parcels at dizzying prices. Riven felt like a genius.

Then the first cracks appeared.

A delay in the builder engine. A sudden token dip. A few influencers grew silent. Marketplace volume dropped. The bright excitement that had filled the servers turned into quiet confusion.

Riven checked his parcel. Its estimated value had dropped 20%. Then 40%. Then 60%.

He told himself not to panic. "It'll recover," he whispered.

But days later, rumors spread: the developers had disappeared. The official social accounts went dark. Users tried to reassure each other—until the truth emerged.

LumaVerse wasn't a metaverse revolution. It was a coordinated scam.

Riven stared at the screen in shock. The parcel he bought at a premium was worthless. His crypto wallet showed the devastating loss in cold numbers. The avatars he once saw celebrating in LumaVerse stood silent, wandering an empty world abandoned by its creators.

He felt embarrassed. Angry with them—but even angrier with himself. He had ignored every red flag: no real roadmap, unverified screenshots, flashy marketing with no substance, founders who refused to appear in interviews. He had traded strategy for excitement.

For a while, Riven considered quitting digital real estate altogether. The loss stung deeply—not just financially, but emotionally. The metaverse no longer felt like a place of opportunity. It felt dangerous, unpredictable, hostile.

Then, one night, he visited a quiet corner of Decentraland, standing on a simple parcel he had bought weeks earlier—one he had researched properly. It belonged to a stable district, surrounded by active creators, close to an upcoming event zone. He remembered how confident and calm he felt when he bought it. Not excited—just certain.

A thought entered his mind:

"I did it right here. I can do it right again."

That night, he made a promise to himself: he would become the kind of investor who could foresee scams, evaluate worlds with precision, spot red flags instantly, and protect others from the mistakes he made.

And he kept that promise.

He studied platform governance, smart contract verification, developer backgrounds, token metrics, on-chain activity, and market cycles. He learned to identify hype patterns and the signs of manipulation. He became active in trusted communities. He helped newcomers avoid dangerous worlds. Slowly, he rebuilt his portfolio—carefully, intelligently, without emotion.

Months later, Riven stood on another parcel—this one in a thriving world with strong adoption—and watched as visitors explored the district he helped develop. His land had doubled in value. Then tripled. His income returned stronger than before.

The loss from LumaVerse never disappeared, but it transformed him. It made him wiser, sharper, more disciplined. He no longer chased noise. He chased signals.

Riven learned what all successful digital real estate investors eventually discover:

The metaverse rewards the informed, not the impulsive. The patient, not the panicked. The strategic, not the speculative.

The parcel that almost destroyed him became the lesson that built his future.

Chapter 10

Advanced Wealth Strategies: Portfolio Building, Estate Management & Long-Term Appreciation

Once you understand how to buy, flip, rent, and develop digital land, the next step is evolving from individual transactions into a long-term strategic portfolio. A portfolio turns scattered parcels into a unified wealth engine capable of generating appreciation, passive income, brand opportunities, and scalable digital influence. Advanced portfolio building is not about owning the most land—it is about owning the *right* land, arranged with purpose, diversified for stability, and structured for multi-decade growth. In the same way traditional real estate investors progress from single properties to multi-unit portfolios, digital real estate investors must learn how to manage estates, clusters, revenue funnels, and appreciation cycles. Chapter 10 provides a complete blueprint for building, managing, protecting, and optimizing a metaverse property portfolio that can stand strong through market shifts and technological evolution.

The first principle of a wealth-building portfolio is **strategic diversification**, which differs from random dispersal.

Diversification means owning parcels across multiple worlds, distinct districts, various risk categories, and different income models. For example, you may own one rental property in Decentraland, one flipping parcel in The Sandbox, one long-term hold in Otherside, and one development-heavy parcel in Spatial. Diversification protects you from platform risk, token fluctuations, and seasonal demand cycles. Each world has different adoption patterns; by spreading your assets, you balance volatility with stability.

The second principle is **category balancing**, ensuring your portfolio includes multiple asset types: – **Appreciation-based parcels** in high-growth districts – **Cash-flow parcels** optimized for rentals – **Development-ready parcels** suited for businesses or experiences – **Speculative parcels** in early-stage worlds – **Liquid parcels** near portals or roads for fast resale Each category plays a role. Appreciation parcels grow wealth over years. Rentals generate monthly cash flow. Development parcels boost long-term value. Speculative parcels deliver high-risk, high-reward opportunities. Liquid parcels act as short-term cash engines. A balanced portfolio gives you every advantage at once.

The third advanced strategy is **estate-building**, which involves merging adjacent parcels to create large multi-unit estates. Estates are far more valuable than individual parcels because they allow: – large-scale businesses – multi-room experiences – full interaction zones – branded installations – event complexes – layered monetization models Estates attract brands, developers, and high-paying tenants. They also appreciate faster because they are scarce. Most worlds have limited clusters of adjacent parcels available; as time passes, estates become highly coveted. Even combining two or three parcels can significantly increase portfolio strength.

A fourth key element is **district specialization**, which means becoming a recognized expert or presence in a particular district. Some investors choose to dedicate a portion of their portfolio to a single niche—art districts, fashion zones, gaming hubs, business centers, or education corridors. This specialization deepens your understanding of demand patterns, tenant desires, event schedules, and development trends. It also increases your influence; district communities quickly recognize consistent contributors, creating opportunities for collaboration, governance roles, and brand partnerships.

Another powerful strategy is **value stacking**, where multiple monetization methods are layered on the same property. For example, a parcel may: – host ticketed events – rent weekday classroom space – display gallery art for commission – sell branded wearables – generate advertising revenue – offer VIP access upgrades This stacking multiplies income beyond simple rent or appreciation. Digital property can support more revenue streams than physical property because the environment itself is programmable. High-performing portfolios master value stacking to maximize output per parcel.

The sixth advanced strategy is **cycle optimization**, where investors buy aggressively during quiet cycles and sell selectively during hype cycles. In downturn phases, land is abundant and prices are discounted; long-term visionaries accumulate strategically. In hype waves—after platform updates, major events, or mainstream announcements—prices can surge suddenly. Portfolio owners can sell certain parcels at peak prices to reinvest into undervalued assets elsewhere. Cycle optimization ensures continuous compounding rather than stagnant holding.

Next is **estate utility development**, which involves upgrading your largest parcels with high-utility builds that compound in value. A vacant estate is an asset; a developed estate is a magnet. Adding modular venues, lounge spaces, educational zones, or interactive experiences transforms estates into income machines. Large estates also attract brand activations, paid partnerships, sponsorships, and permanent tenants—unlocking higher rates and multi-month contracts. Utility is the amplifier of estate value. Another advanced wealth-building approach is **cross-world synergy**, where your properties across different platforms support each other. A gallery in Decentraland may link to your showroom in Spatial. A game in The Sandbox can promote your venue in Otherside. A VR classroom in Somnium Space can showcase your art district estates. Cross-world linking creates a unified digital empire rather than disconnected properties. This synergy increases visibility, user flow, and brand recognition.

The ninth pillar of long-term strategy is **portfolio automation**, which becomes essential as your holdings grow. Automating rentals, payments, permissions, visitor analytics, event scheduling, and maintenance ensures you manage your portfolio efficiently without daily manual involvement. Automation reduces stress, improves consistency, and ensures your portfolio generates wealth even while you're away.

Finally, the core of every advanced portfolio is **vision-driven appreciation**. Digital land is an early-stage asset class. Its long-term value will be shaped by technological progress, mainstream adoption, AI evolution, cross-platform interoperability, and the future of digital identity. Investors who build portfolios with a 5–15-year vision, rather than a 5–15-day mindset, will benefit the most. Strong portfolios weather cycles, capitalize on innovation, and position themselves as foundational pillars in emerging worlds. Digital real estate is not just a short-term opportunity—it is a generational wealth vehicle for those who approach it with strategy, discipline, and imagination.

"The Architect of Three Worlds"

Kade never set out to build a digital empire. He only wanted one good parcel—something quiet, something simple. But the metaverse had other plans for him.

It started with his first parcel in The Sandbox, a small corner lot near a creator hub. He built a minimal workshop there, a place to experiment with assets. He didn't think much of it. Over time, creators visited, asked questions, and complimented the space. Encouraged, Kade bought a second parcel—this time in Decentraland, inside an art district. He rented it out occasionally, then built a gallery, then expanded with an event room. His parcels weren't random acquisitions—they naturally reflected the worlds he loved.

But something changed the day he bought his third parcel in Otherside.

That parcel was different. It wasn't just land; it was a frontier. Floating islands glowed beneath swirling skies. Creatures roamed with bioluminescent fur. The energy felt electric, alive, powerful. Kade knew instantly that this wasn't just another investment—this was the foundation of something bigger.

He stood on the new parcel and asked himself a question he had never considered:

"What if I built across all three worlds—not separately, but together?"

That question sparked the birth of The TriVerse Project.

He began by expanding his Sandbox workshop into a full creator academy—tutorial rooms, testing spaces, collaborative tables, and modular buildings. He linked it to his Decentraland gallery through teleportation portals. Artists could visit the gallery, then jump directly into Sandbox to build something, then continue to Otherside for immersive exploration.

Next, he expanded his Decentraland estate by acquiring two adjacent parcels. He merged them into a multi-room cultural center—gallery, lounge, music hall, and marketplace. He then added holographic maps pointing to his other worlds.

Finally, he transformed his Otherside parcel into a lush sanctuary with floating bridges, flying creatures, and interactive energy wells. It wasn't a build—it was a living dream. When visitors explored the sanctuary, they found portals that led back to the gallery and the creator academy.

And then visitors began to arrive.

First dozens, then hundreds, then thousands.

Creators traveled through his spaces daily. Artists hosted exhibitions in Decentraland. Developers trained in Sandbox. Explorers meditated in Otherside. Kade didn't just build properties—he built an interconnected digital universe.

Soon, brands reached out. Schools wanted to host workshops. Musicians wanted to perform. Gaming clans wanted to run collaborative events. His spaces became known as "The TriVerse"—a trilogy of worlds connected through creativity, exploration, and community.

One evening, standing on the floating cliffs of his Otherside sanctuary, Kade looked down at visitors wandering the glowing paths. Every corner was alive with laughter, movement, and light. His Discord buzzed with artists planning exhibitions, creators suggesting upgrades, and explorers sharing discoveries.

He whispered to himself, "I built this. All of it."

Not because he bought the most land. Not because he chased hype. But because he saw what others didn't: the power of connection. A portfolio that wasn't a collection—but a universe.

As he watched the visitors teleport from one world to another, Kade understood something profound:

Digital real estate wasn't about owning land. It was about designing worlds. It was about building legacies. It was about becoming an architect of the future.

And Kade, the quiet investor who only wanted one good parcel, had become exactly that.

Epilogue

The metaverse is no longer a distant dream or a speculative experiment; it is a living, evolving frontier that bridges imagination with opportunity in ways humanity has never experienced before. As you reach the end of this book, understand that you are standing at the beginning of one of the greatest technological and economic shifts of our era. Digital real estate is not just about buying virtual parcels or creating immersive experiences—it is about participating in a transformation of value, ownership, culture, and identity that will define the future of how we work, learn, create, socialize, and build wealth. What you now understand is something millions still haven't realized: the digital world is not secondary to the physical world anymore; it is quickly becoming its own universe with rules, economies, and opportunities that are expanding exponentially.

Throughout these chapters, you learned how digital land functions, why it holds value, and how it can be leveraged for both short-term and long-term wealth. You explored the mechanics of buying, flipping, and renting parcels. You discovered how to identify high-demand districts, how to avoid scams, how to analyze communities, and how to evaluate platform longevity. You learned the strategies professional investors use to build scalable portfolios, merge parcels into estates, create modular builds, layer income streams, and develop long-term appreciation cycles. You saw how ordinary creators turned simple parcels into thriving businesses. You learned how visibility, marketing, collaboration, and experiential design transform digital property into living attractions that people return to again and again. And perhaps most importantly, you have grown into someone who sees beyond the hype—someone who can analyze, strategize, build, and invest with clarity and confidence.

The metaverse is still early. Early like the internet was in the 1990s. Early like social media was in 2008. Early like mobile apps, NFTs, crypto, and AI were before mass adoption. The early phase of every technological revolution always belongs to innovators—the ones who are willing to learn, observe, adapt, and take action before the world fully understands what is happening. The land you buy today, the experiences you build now, the collaborations you form, the communities you join, and the strategies you apply will shape your position years from now. This is how early pioneers in traditional real estate, domain investing, social media branding, and cryptocurrency built fortunes that multiplied exponentially as mainstream adoption caught up.

As more users enter digital worlds—through VR headsets, AR glasses, smartphones, gaming systems, and future wearable technologies—digital land will become premium real estate. Brands will establish headquarters. Musicians will build concert arenas. Educators will run virtual campuses. Businesses will open storefronts. AI agents will manage experiences and services 24/7. Digital identity will become as important as physical identity. Digital ownership will be as respected as physical ownership. And those who positioned themselves early will be the ones who thrive the most.

Your role now is to decide the type of digital real estate investor or creator you want to be. Will you specialize in one world or build across many? Will you rent parcels, create experiences, develop event venues, build commercial districts, or design immersive environments for brands? Will you construct a portfolio that generates long-term passive income? Will you flip premium parcels during hype cycles? Will you become a district leader, a gallery owner, a virtual architect, a game designer, or a metaverse developer? The possibilities are endless—but all of them begin with the same foundation: ownership, creativity, and strategic execution.

Do not underestimate the power of small actions. The first parcel you buy may one day become the foundation of a digital empire. The first experience you build may evolve into a landmark. The first collaboration you form may become the alliance that pushes your digital brand into the mainstream. Every major success story begins with a beginner who decided to start. And starting today gives you an advantage that millions who enter later will never have.

The metaverse belongs to the bold, the curious, and the visionary. And now, equipped with the knowledge in this book, you are no longer an observer—you are an architect of your digital destiny. You have the tools, strategies, and understanding to build something extraordinary. The landscape is wide open. The opportunities are limitless. The next chapter of digital wealth creation is unfolding, and you are standing at the doorway of the future.

So step forward. Build. Create. Invest. Explore. Shape. Innovate. Become a pioneer in this new frontier. One day, as the metaverse becomes a fully integrated part of everyday life, you will look back and know you were early—you understood the future before the world did.

And that is the greatest advantage anyone can ever have.

www.ingramcontent.com/pod-product-compliance
Ingram Content Group UK Ltd.
Pitfield, Milton Keynes, MK11 3LW, UK
UKHW020158290926
15471UKWH00005B/932

9 798295 491191